Foreword

Singing ('umculo') is a huge part of the culture and everyday life of ↑
so than those in Southern Africa. The first song in this volume, *Ha*
advises Lulu, a bride, to 'Hush, listen to all the things they are telling
is in fact incredibly straightforward, with a gentle, comforting rhythn
It then follows with the choir and soloist (or group of singers) intoni
men of the choir and then the sopranos take over this tune in the n
softly as you dare, with humming.

C000300201

Rather like *Hamba Lulu*, *Jesu ukukhanya* has a call-and-response structure. Its simple solo line is followed
by a choral answer that, typically of this style of music, moves predominantly in parallel harmony. The
words first boldly proclaim that Jesus is the light, and then that 'we' and 'you' are also. Pronounce it
'Ye-soo oo-koo-kan-ya' and, in the second verse, 'See-pett'. The song gives the chance for a variety of
singers to have a go at the solo part, at any octave! We've given some suggestions for dynamics, but
encourage your soloist to try varying them, with the choir copying the dynamic chosen. The
arrangement also works unaccompanied.

A joyful, exuberant song with an infectious rhythm, *Si njay njay njay* is easy to learn, as it builds up
gradually from just the men, and then men and altos, to all three parts. The second-verse notes are the
same, but watch out for the changes of rhythm on 'Woh mama bagu…' and 'babay thanda zah'
('thanda' is pronounced with a hard 't'). The optional percussion adds a great deal to this number and,
when you are more confident with the notes, you can also sing it completely *a cappella* – that is, without
the piano. Just set the percussion groove going and start singing!

Weeping is a South African pop song that was recorded in 1987 by a band called Bright Blue. It calls out
against the injustices of Apartheid Government and uses as its chorus the refrain from the Zulu anthem
'N'kosi Sikeleli Africa' ('God bless Africa'), which had been banned by the South African National Party.
'Thina lusapholwayo' ('God bless us, her children') is pronounced with a hard 't'. The 'sing out' section
starts tentatively but soon grows to a collective, gospel-style chorus. If you have some bass singers and
would like to try some four-part harmony, there is an opportunity to thicken the texture (with the small
notes written in the men's part) in the final chorus – you could even to try it *a cappella*, for an authentic
sound!

These wonderful African songs are just four of the many that have been sung or taught to me over the
years by a number of friends, and I hope you enjoy learning, singing and performing them as much as
I have. They are the kind of songs that are difficult to sing while sitting or standing still: they were never
intended for formal concert performance, but rather for communal music-making, story-telling or
celebration. Allow your bodies to move, or feel free to clap or click: perhaps on beats 2 and 4 for *Jesu, Si
njay* and *Weeping*. *Hamba Lulu* has its own traditional movement pattern that you might like to try: the
left foot (followed by the left hip) gently stamps or presses down on beat one (the soloist's 'Hamba') and
the right foot and hip do the same on beat three-and-a-half (the chorus's 'Hamba'); effectively dividing
the bar in half and setting up a lovely, slow sideways-rocking motion.

Alexander L'Estrange, March 2004

Editorial notes

Choral Basics has been devised to provide arrangements and original pieces specifically for beginner
choirs.

Vocal ranges: the arrangements don't explore the extremes of the voice, but aim to stretch the vocal
range from time to time in the context of a well-placed musical phrase. Small notes indicate optional
alternatives: 1) where the main notes may fall out of comfortable range for some singers, 2) where
certain singers on the male-voice part, which mainly falls in the baritone range of a 10th (B–D), wish
to explore the tenor or bass register, or 3) where a doubling within a part is suggested.

Breathing: singers should aim to follow the punctuation of the text, and breathe accordingly. However,
commas above the music suggest places to breathe where not provided for within the text.

Piano accompaniments: the simple yet imaginative piano parts have been written to support the vocal
lines. Small notes in the piano part are intended to help support singers while learning the piece;
however, once more confident you may choose to omit the notes, or just to play them very gently.

Hamba Lulu

Zulu traditional
arr. Alexander L'Estrange

6

SOLO (or semichorus)

Ham-ba Lu -lu,___ ham-ba Lu -lu,___ ham-ba Lu -lu,___
mm___ mm___ mm___

S. A.

-lu, ham-ba Lu - lu, ham-ba Lu - lu, ham-ba Lu -
-lu. mm___ mm___ mm___

MEN

ham-ba Lu - lu, ham-ba Lu - lu, ham-ba Lu -
(- lu.) mm___ mm___ mm___

p (2. **pp**)

poco rit. (*2nd time only*)

ham-ba Lu - lu.___ O ham-ba Lu - lu.___
mm___ mm___ mm

-lu, ham-ba Lu - lu, ham-ba Lu -
— mm___ mm___

-lu, ham-ba Lu - lu, ham-ba Lu -
— mm___ mm___

poco rit. (*2nd time only*)

Jesu ukukhanya

Botswana traditional
arr. Alexander L'Estrange

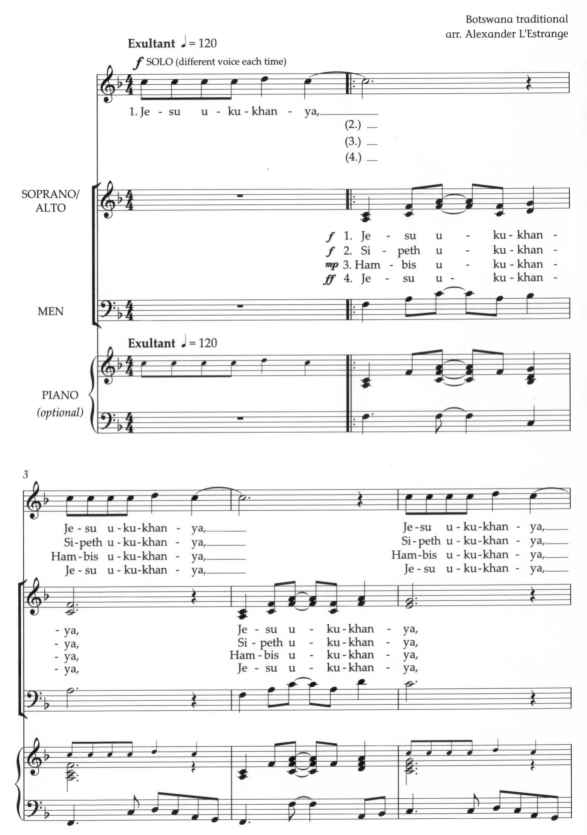

Si njay njay njay

Zulu traditional
arr. Alexander L'Estrange

* use shakers and 2 bongos, or similar

10

* use shakers and 2 bongos, or similar

14

Weeping
(N'kosi Sikeleli Africa)

Dan Heymann
arr. Alexander L'Estrange

16

* change gradually from yo to *mm*

* Some men may sing this second, lower part.